the LAST YEARS of the 'WESTERNS'

A.WYN HOBSON

LONDON
IAN ALLAN LTD

Cover: An unidentified 'Western' runs into Par station with a Paddington-Penzance train in October 1974. *Derek Cross*

Back cover top: No 1048 *Western Lady* heads an up mineral train under the former Barry Railway viaduct near St Fagans, Cardiff, on 8 September 1973. *A. Wyn Hobson*

Back cover bottom: No 1052 *Western Viceroy* heads a down parcels train past West Ealing on 11 September 1972. *A. Wyn Hobson*

Previous page: No 1001 *Western Pathfinder* approaches Dainton summit with the 08.30 Paddington-Penzance on 6 August 1971. *J. H. Cooper-Smith*

First published 1983

ISBN 0 7110 1282 2

Published by Ian Allan Ltd, Shepperton, Surrey; and printed by Ian Allan Printing Ltd at their works at Coombelands in Runnymede, England

Introduction

Just what *were* 'the last years of the Westerns'? To ask this question is to realise that it presents possibilities for one of those zestfully pedantic differences of opinion so beloved of locomotive enthusiasts — in this case, as to exactly what was the point at which 'The End' began. Was it 1976, when Swindon Works finally ceased all spare-part repairs for the Class 52s? Hardly — well over half the class had already been withdrawn from service by then. Was it 1975, when it was announced that the class would all be withdrawn by year's end, and the photographers began to turn out in earnest in pursuit of the remaining examples? Or was it 1973, when Swindon undertook the last major overhaul of a 'Western', and the first withdrawals took place? For a good many younger enthusiasts, it was very probably then ; yet to those few of us, of an older generation, who had been fascinated by these locomotives ever since that first photograph of D1000, painted in a strange light-coloured livery and hauling a parcels train through Iver, had leapt out at us from the pages of the February 1962 issue of *Modern Railways*, the somewhat surprised realisation that the class would soon be going the way of the steam locomotive had surely come sooner than 1973.

Was the moment, then, 1971, when the South Wales allocation of 52s was abruptly removed to Plymouth Laira depot, and it was announced that the class would be swiftly phased out of South Wales service? No — was it not, rather, 1970: when the D6xx 'Warships' locomotives were already extinct, the little North British-built D63xx B-Bs and the ill-conceived Swindon D95xx 0-6-0s considerably depleted, and gaps already appearing in the roll of the D8xx 'Warships'; and the decision was finally made that the 'Westerns' and the 'Hymek' class were soon to follow those other main line diesel-hydraulic types. Yes; that, surely, was the real turning-point: the moment at which one began to watch 'Westerns' in that special way that is born of the knowledge that the sight will soon be no longer possible — will soon be another element of the world of one's youth that has vanished for ever. The moment at which one began to feel that every photograph of a 'Western' must, if possible, be a *good* photograph — conveying something of its power, or of its distinctive life and shape in a landscape — and not just another routine record-shot.

The end, though, was an astonishingly long time coming. The Marylebone Road administrators who decided on the class's early demise little imagined that, because of delays in the Western Region's traction modernisation and an upsurge in freight traffic, the 'Westerns' as a class were still only a little beyond the half-way point of what would prove to be their eventual service-life. My own memory of the period is one of repeated false alarms. I was a student in South Wales at the time, several times impelled into fresh photographic efforts by announcements that the 'Westerns' would finally disappear from the area at the end of the current timetable-period. But it never seemed to work out like that in practice — a sprinkling of appearances by 52s continued on the Paddington-Swansea services (though few of the workings were regularly diagrammed); and because of BR's diehard habit of rostering Mark I coaching-stock for boat-trains, 'Westerns' were working even as far west as Fishguard until only a few months before the last examples were withdrawn.

Local rumour had it that all this had not a little to do with the fact that Cardiff Canton, despite having lost its official allocation of 52s, was one of the only two depots possessed of the facilities for carrying out certain types of heavy maintenance on the class. Perhaps, on the other hand, it was simply that the Operating Department maintained an obstinate affection for these mechanically rather resilient locomotives. Certainly the 1975 decision to confine the 52s to freight duties only was ignored in practice, to the very end; and the last years of the 'Westerns' saw them operating sporadic express passenger trains on all except the Bristol and Worcester main lines until a very late stage.

Freight and parcels work, however, did come to figure more and more largely in the class's operations during the years (1970-77) covered by this volume. Several of the photographs in this collection bear witness, too, to the inevitable decline in the locomotives' mechanical and external condition. Others, on the other hand, remind one strikingly of how much, visually speaking as well as in other respects, the 'Westerns' were an aspect of a scene which still savoured strongly, in parts, of the former GWR, with its lower-quadrant signals and distinctively designed signalboxes and rolling-stock — artefacts which today have vanished almost as completely as the 'Westerns' themselves from the Western Region's main lines.

As well as attempting to present something of these facets of the scene during the last years of the 'Westerns', I have tried to do some measure of justice to the many different ways in which we physically *saw* them. The ground- or platform-level front three-quarter photograph of a train or locomotive, with background thoroughly subordinated, is a pictorial convention born of the inflexibility of heavy Victorian and Edwardian camera-equipment, and presents what is in fact only a limited and specialised version of what we see when we look at a railway system. Thus it is that this volume emphasises the contexts — landscape and other — in which the 'Westerns' worked in their last years, and does so by means of a variety of pictorial approaches. I have also, in this selection, purposely avoided most of the well-known WR locations and viewpoints popular with generations of railway-photographers, and well represented in other, previous volumes on the Class 52s; and I have deliberately devoted only limited space to that extraordinary spate of 'farewell' railtours in 1976-77, which have been portrayed so compendiously by other hands. My hope in fact has been to add by extension, rather than duplication, to the permanent collective memory of the 'Western' locomotives in their fraying yet tumultuous final period: to put on record a little more of the feel of the way it was, and the way they were.

A. Wyn Hobson

Above: An impression of the might of the 'Westerns', as No 1069 *Western Vanguard* hurls an up express past Twyford on 20 July 1974. *Geoff Dowling*

Left: An unidentified 'Western' speeds through Ealing Broadway station with an up express on 9 September 1972. *A. Wyn Hobson*

Above right: No 1065 *Western Consort* appears to be 'in steam' at Paddington! Presumably a train-heating pipe had either fractured or become disconnected. *Geoff Pinder*

Right: The dramatic cloud of exhaust put up by No 1054 *Western Governor*, as it leaves Swindon with the 09.03 Swansea-Paddington on 22 February 1975, betokens the declining standards of maintenance on the class in their last years. *T. G. Flinders*

Left: No 1063 *Western Monitor* runs light into Ranelagh Road locomotive yard after working an express into Paddington on a bright day in August 1974. *Peter Dobson*

Right: No 1037 *Western Empress* passes Paddington parcels depot as it leaves with the summer Saturday 09.50 for Newquay on 8 May 1976. *John Vaughan*

Below: No 1058 *Western Nobleman* accelerates forcefully out of Truro with the 12.50 Penzance-Crewe parcels train on 27 November 1974. *Brian Morrison*

Below far right: No 1072 *Western Glory*, working empty coaching stock out of Paddington, approaches Old Oak Common depot in June 1973. *Peter Dobson*

4M 05

D 1072

An unidentified 'Western' passes Westbourne Park station with an up South Wales express on 1 May 1970.
Michael Baker

Above: No 1062 *Western Courier* passes Westbourne Park with empty stock for Old Oak Common on 21 March 1970.
A. Wyn Hobson

Below: On the rather hazy, overcast afternoon of 2 September 1975, No 1005 *Western Venturer* approaches Paddington with the 10.25 from Birmingham New Street. *G. Scott-Lowe*

Left: An unidentified 'Western' is seen crossing the graceful arches of Brunel's Hanwell Viaduct with the 14.30 Paddington-Paignton on 8 November 1972.
J. H. Cooper-Smith

Right: A view, from the front coach of the 16.05 Paddington-Birmingham, of No 1053 *Western Patriarch* at speed under a dramatic autumn sky on 21 October 1976.
Peter Walton

Below: No 1032 *Western Marksman* heads the 10.30 Paddington-Paignton through West Ealing station on 11 September 1972. *A. Wyn Hobson*

Below: Milk trains between London and the West Country and South Wales were long a feature of the GWR and Western Region scene, and after the demise of the 'Hymek' diesel-hydraulics, 'Western' locomotives saw a good deal of service on these trains. Here a down working passes Highworth Junction, Swindon, behind No 1071 *Western Renown* on 16 April 1976. *T. G. Flinders*

Bottom: On the showery afternoon of 24 February 1977, only three days before the withdrawal from service of the last five members of the 'Western' class, No 1048 *Western Lady* heads the returning 'Western Lament' special train past Swindon Works. *T. G. Flinders*

Above: No 1041 *Western Prince* picks its way past a snowbound Swindon station with a down hopper train on the morning of 17 December 1976. *T. G. Flinders*

Below left: After high-speed running through a blizzard with the 10.40 Paddington-Plymouth on 13 January 1977, the front end of No 1013 *Western Ranger* is encrusted with snow and ice as it pauses at Westbury. *Philip D. Hawkins*

Below: Another view of No 1013 *Western Ranger* pausing at Westbury with the 10.40 Paddington-Plymouth on 13 January 1977. *Philip D. Hawkins*

Left: On a misty May morning in 1971, No 1053 *Western Patriarch* heads the 06.35 Penzance-Paddington past Witham signalbox, Somerset. *G. F. Gillham*

Above: On a very wet 17 May 1976, No 1041 *Western Prince* arrives at Truro with the 09.30 Paddington-Penzance. *John Vaughan*

Right: On a bright, cold winter morning in November 1974, No 1012 *Western Firebrand* speeds past Lavington signalbox, near Westbury, with the 09.30 Paddington-Penzance. *G. F. Gillham*

Above: No 1068 *Western Reliance* passes Hungerford with a New Year relief to the 09.30 Paddington-Penzance on 3 January 1976. *T. G. Flinders*

Left: Ex-GWR semaphore signals and notices are prominent in this view of No 1049 *Western Monarch* east of Hungerford with the 07.53 Paignton-Paddington on 2 March 1976. *T. G. Flinders*

Above right: The powerful chemicals used in Western Region washing-plants tended to have a particularly corrosive effect on locomotive paintwork. Here a very worn-looking No 1001 *Western Pathfinder* leaves Dawlish Warren with a Paignton-Exeter local on 19 August 1975. *Roger Kaye*

Right: No 1028 *Western Hussar* waits for a clear road at a gantry of ex-GWR semaphore signals at Aller Junction, Newton Abbot, on 19 June 1975. *T. G. Flinders*

PASS ICERS
ARE NO ALLOWED
CROSS E RAILWAY
CEPT B E BRIDGE
6Z 63

The first of the 'Westerns', No 1000 *Western Enterprise*, is glimpsed between the trees by the Kennet and Avon Canal as it climbs towards Savernake summit with the 13.30 Paddington–Penzance on 6 June 1973.
J. H. Cooper-Smith

Above: Sweeping downhill near Great Bedwyn, Wiltshire, is No 1065 *Western Consort* at the head of the 11.00 Plymouth-Paddington on 15 April 1976. *John Vaughan*

Below: No 1057 *Western Chieftain* approaches Crofton curve with the 14.30 Paddington-Paignton on the misty afternoon of 6 February 1975. *Philip D. Hawkins*

92

Left: In their later years, the 'Westerns' saw a period of service on the Bristol-Weymouth route. On the chilly, damp morning of 9 February 1975, No 1055 *Western Advocate* is at the head of the 10.05 for Bristol at Weymouth; on the right a 4-TC unit heads a train for Waterloo. *Michael Baker*

Centre left: The paradoxically-named No 1056 *Western Sultan* is glimpsed from a distance at the head of an eastbound stone-train at Westbury, in appropriately simmering conditions on 21 July 1975. Nearby, a Class 46 awaits its next duty. *D. Griffiths*

Bottom left: A down West of England express leaves Westbury behind an unidentified 'Western' on a misty day in March 1973. *Michael Baker*

Right: No 1022 *Western Sentinel*, at rest between stone-train duties, stands reflected in a stagnant pool outside Westbury locomotive depot in April 1976. *John Chalcraft*

Below: No 1013 *Western Ranger* (left) and No 1001 *Western Pathfinder* at Westbury depot on 20 April 1975. *G. Scott-Lowe*

Right: No 1071 *Western Renown* shunts at Merehead Stone Quarry, Somerset, on 18 February 1975. *G. Scott-Lowe*

Below: Country road-traffic waits at Latteridge crossing as No 1072 *Western Glory* makes for Tytherington Quarry, on the former Midland Railway Yate-Thornbury branch, near Bristol, with a train of stone empties on 14 July 1976. *G. Scott-Lowe*

Above left: An unidentified 'Western' with an express near Crofton.
T. G. Flinders

Above: No 1065 *Western Consort* heads away from Salisbury Tunnel Junction on to the Romsey line, with a Westbury-Fareham stone train on the morning of 18 March 1975. *G. F. Gillham*

Below: No 1071 *Western Renown* crosses one of Gloucester's many level crossings, at Horton Road, with the Etruria (Stoke-on-Trent)-St Blazey 'Clayliner' empties train on 2 October 1976.
G. Scott-Lowe

A comparison of roof-profiles at Bristol Temple Meads station, as No 1028 *Western Hussar* prepares to leave with the 15.45 for Paddington on 6 August 1973.
J. H. Cooper-Smith

Above: With only one engine working — and poorly at that — No 1048 *Western Lady* leaves Reading with an up parcels train on 3 July 1976. *John Vaughan*

Below: No 1068 *Western Reliance* pauses at Reading with the 17.30 *'Golden Hind'* Paddington-Penzance express on 17 July 1976. *John Vaughan*

Above: No 1054 *Western Governor* runs light into North Road station, Plymouth, to work the 11.30 from Paddington forward to Penzance on 24 July 1976. *John Vaughan*

Left: No 1041 *Western Prince* runs light towards Laira locomotive depot for refuelling on 23 July 1976, after arrival at Plymouth on a down parcels working. *John Vaughan*

Right: No 1046 *Western Marquis* starts away from Paignton with the 16.25 for Paddington on 6 September 1975. *Philip D. Hawkins*

CINEMA
TORBAY STEAM RAILWAY
TAXIS
D 1046
BARCLAYS

Above left: With the sun setting over Dartmoor, No 1058 *Western Nobleman* passes the site of the former South Brent station with the daily St Erth-Acton milk train on 13 August 1976. *Les Bertram*

Left: No 1028 *Western Hussar* begins the long climb up Rattery Bank, near Newton Abbott, with a parcels train on 4 August 1976. *Les Bertram*

Above: No 1015 *Western Champion* coasts into Totnes with an express on 6 September 1975. *Geoff Dowling*

Right: An unidentified 'Western' passes the Bathampton loops, with their array of semaphore signals, as it slows for the Bath stop with the 13.45 Paddington-Bristol on 4 May 1970. The Bristol route was the first to lose its 'Western'-hauled passenger services to High Speed Trains. *J. H. Cooper-Smith*

Top: A 'Western' heads a Paddington-Penzance express out of Exeter on 25 September 1974. *R. Elsdon*

Above centre: No 1068 *Western Reliance* passes Torre with the 15.55 Paignton-Paddington on 21 August 1974. *Les Bertram*

Above: No 1068 *Western Reliance* climbs past Treffery viaduct, in the Luxulyan Valley, with the summer Saturday 09.50 Paddington-Newquay on 5 June 1976. *Les Bertram*

Right: No 1071 *Western Renown*, glimpsed with a St Austell-Kensington Olympia motorail train in the West Country in July 1975. *D. Griffiths*

Right: No 1023 *Western Fusilier* awaits the right-away with a down express at Exeter St Davids on 10 September 1974.
A. O. Wynn

Below: Both paintwork and engines of No 1065 *Western Consort* are showing signs of considerable wear as it stands idling at Exeter St Davids on 18 September 1976.
John Vaughan

Left: No 1047 *Western Lord* pauses at Dawlish with a Paddington-Paignton service on a damp May morning in 1972. *A. O. Wynn*

Below: Conversation-piece at Exeter St Davids on 29 March 1975, as No 1036 *Western Emperor* awaits its next turn of duty. *A. O. Wynn*

Above: A notable feature of West Country freight traffic has long been the china clay trains to and from Cornwall, and these workings were often entrusted to 'Westerns' in their later years. Here No 1071 *Western Renown* passes Cockwood harbour, near Dawlish Warren, with a train consisting mainly of clay empties, on 4 August 1976. *Les Bertram*

Below: No 1041 *Western Prince* heads the 09.35 Paddington-Penzance past Mounts Bay in September 1970. *Michael Baker*

Above right: A lone spectator on the sea-front at Dawlish watches as the 09.30 Paddington-Penzance, headed by No 1023 *Western Fusilier*, slows to a halt at an adverse signal on 7 September 1974. *A. O. Wynn*

Right: The 'Westerns', during the mid-1970s, regularly worked the St Blazey-Etruria (Stoke-on-Trent) china clay trains as far as Bescot Yard in the West Midlands. On 21 May 1976, No 1041 *Western Prince* threads the sea-wall curves at Teignmouth with the return empties working. *John Whitehouse*

Above: On a hazy afternoon in April 1976, No 1048 *Western Lady* leaves Teignmouth with an up parcels train. *D. Griffiths*

Left: No 1053 *Western Patriarch* stands near the sea-wall at Teignmouth in April 1976 with a permanent-way maintenance train. *D. Griffiths*

Right: A 'Western' hauls a down express over St Germans viaduct on 23 July 1973. *J. H. Cooper-Smith*

Above: No 1023 *Western Fusilier*, glimpsed on a china clay train at St Blazey locomotive depot during a torrential downpour on 19 May 1976. *John Vaughan*

Below: No 1004 *Western Crusader* approaches Lostwithiel station with an express in July 1975, passing a Class 25 hurrying away in the opposite direction. *D. Griffiths*

Top: No 1047 *Western Lord* stands idling in sidings near Exeter St Davids on 22 September 1974. *R. Elsdon*

Above: Milk tankers await their next duty as an unidentified 'Western' pauses at Totnes with an express on a hot day in July 1975. *D. Griffiths*

Top: No 1054 *Western Governor* pauses at Exeter St Davids with a Bristol-Plymouth train on the night of 24 September 1974. *R. Elsdon*

Above: One of Westbury depot's few remaining passenger turns, by the mid-1970s, was the 06.40 semi-fast for Paddington. Here No 1048 *Western Lady* prepares for departure on the morning of 4 February 1977. *G. Scott-Lowe*

Above: No 1013 *Western Ranger* stands in the departure line at Bristol Bath Road locomotive depot, waiting to take over the 19.15 service for Plymouth on the night of 6 February 1977.
G. Scott-Lowe

Above right: On a wet February evening in 1976, No 1072 *Western Glory* pauses at Taunton with the 14.40 Penzance-Paddington.
John Whitehouse

Below: One of the last trains worked by No 1041 *Western Prince* was an inter-regional service, here photographed at Gloucester on a wet evening in January 1977. *John Vaughan*

Above: No 1040 *Western Queen* breasts the summit of Dainton Bank with a Penzance-Paddington express on 6 August 1971.
J. H. Cooper-Smith

Left: Reduced standards of maintenance frequently left 'Westerns' having to work on only one of their two engines in their later years. Here No 1012 *Western Firebrand* pauses at Totnes on 26 July 1975, to obtain assistance, in the shape of Class 25/3 No 25.307, for tackling the South Devon banks with the 13.20 Liverpool-Plymouth.
D. Griffiths

Right: An unidentified 'Western' roars westward near Swindon with the 17.00 Paddington-Swansea on 25 June 1970.
T. G. Flinders

Left: No 1013 *Western Ranger* leaves Bridgend with the 14.55 Swansea-Paddington on a very overcast bank holiday Saturday, 21 April 1973. *A. Wyn Hobson*

Below: No 1046 *Western Marquis* arrives at Neath with the 18.20 Swansea-Paddington on 29 May 1972. *A. Wyn Hobson*

Right: No 1054 *Western Governor* arrives at Neath with the 15.15 Paddington-Swansea on 29 May 1972. *A. Wyn Hobson*

Below right: No 1065 *Western Consort* heads out of Newport station with the 13.15 Paddington-Cardiff on 24 April 1975. *Philip D. Hawkins*

1C81
Inter-City

Above: An unidentified 'Western' passes St George's, near Cardiff, with the 14.53 Swansea-Paddington on 8 September 1973. *A. Wyn Hobson*

Below: A 'Western' heads a down freight past Ely, Cardiff, on 8 September 1973. *A. Wyn Hobson*

Top: No 1032 *Western Marksman* rounds the sharp curve out of Neath and begins the stiff climb of Skewen Bank with the 11.15 Paddington-Cardiff, specially extended to Swansea, on Spring Bank Holiday Monday, 29 May 1972. *A. Wyn Hobson*

Above: No 1007 *Western Talisman* heads the 12.53 Swansea-Paddington past Ely, Cardiff, on 25 August 1973. *A. Wyn Hobson*

Above: No 1053 *Western Patriarch* heads the summer Saturday 09.28 Pembroke Dock-Paddington past Ely, Cardiff, on 25 August 1973. *A. Wyn Hobson*

Below: A 'Western' heads the Saturday 09.15 Paddington-Swansea past Ely, Cardiff, on 25 August 1973. *A. Wyn Hobson*

Above right: No 1025 *Western Guardsman* climbs away from Swansea with an up parcels train on 5 May 1973. *A. Wyn Hobson*

Below right: An unidentified 'Western' passes Briton Ferry, near Neath, with an up block oil train on 10 March 1973. *A. Wyn Hobson*

Above: A 'Western' heads the 10.00 Paddington-Swansea past Pyle, near Bridgend, on 26 May 1973. *A. Wyn Hobson*

Left: An unidentified 'Western' heads the 13.00 Paddington-Swansea past Pencoed, near Bridgend, on 27 May 1974. *A. Wyn Hobson*

Above right: An unidentified 'Western' threads the unusual series of arches on the westward slope of Skewen Bank with the 10.00 Paddington-Swansea on 18 March 1972. *A. Wyn Hobson*

Right: No 1036 *Western Emperor* heads the 13.00 Paddington-Swansea down the bank from Pyle on 26 May 1973. *A. Wyn Hobson*

1C37
1C61

Left: No 1044 *Western Duchess* passes Landore locomotive-depot as it enters Swansea with the 13.00 from Paddington on 14 March 1973. *A. Wyn Hobson*

Below: No 1036 *Western Emperor* passes Llansamlet on its way out of Swansea with the 16.20 for Paddington on 18 March 1972. *A. Wyn Hobson*

Right: No 1037 *Western Empress* passes Briton Ferry with the 11.15 Paddington-Swansea on 10 March 1973. *A. Wyn Hobson*

Below far right: No 1032 *Western Marksman* leaves Neath with the 16.55 Swansea-Paddington on 29 May 1972. *A. Wyn Hobson*

1A71

Above: No 1013 *Western Ranger* passes Llansamlet, Swansea, with the 10.00 from Paddington on 14 February 1972. *A. Wyn Hobson*

Below: An unidentified 'Western' heads the 12.20 Swansea-Paddington past Llansamlet on 18 March 1972. *A. Wyn Hobson*

Top: A 'Western' heads the 12.00 from Paddington past the industrial wastes of the Lower Swansea Valley on 3 June 1972. *A. Wyn Hobson*

Above: No 1004 *Western Crusader* labours up the bank towards Pyle at little more than 5mph with an up coal-train on 26 May 1973. *A. Wyn Hobson*

Above: No 1021 *Western Cavalier* passes Skewen East signalbox, at the summit of Skewen Bank, near Neath, with the 10.00 Paddington-Swansea on 28 October 1972. *A. Wyn Hobson*

Below: No 1024 *Western Huntsman* approaches Swansea with the 11.15 from Paddington on 5 May 1972. *A. Wyn Hobson*

Right: A study of No 1068 *Western Reliance* at the head of the 14.30 for Swansea at Fishguard Harbour, after working in with the 08.25 boat-train from Paddington on 17 June 1976. *John Vaughan*

1068

Seconds before a torrential downpour on 21 April 1973, an unidentified 'Western' runs down into Bridgend with the 15.55 Swansea-Paddington. *A. Wyn Hobson*

Above: No 1013 *Western Ranger* heads the 'Cornishman' special train from Nottingham to Cornwall through Droitwich station in thick fog on 13 November 1976. *R. C. Swift*

Below: No 1066 *Western Prefect* arrives at Swansea with the 12.00 from Paddington on the misty afternoon of 4 December 1971. *A. Wyn Hobson*

Left: No 1023 *Western Fusilier* is 'cabbed' by young enthusiasts at Birmingham New Street after arrival with an express from Paddington on 2 November 1974. *P. J. Shoesmith*

Below: No 1072 *Western Glory* stands at Birmingham New Street between turns on 19 June 1976. *P. J. Shoesmith*

Right: No 1051 *Western Ambassador* is the object of intense interest at Birmingham New Street on 3 May 1975, as the driver prepares it for its return working to Paddington.
R. C. Swift

Below right: No 1067 *Western Druid* waits at Platform 1, Birmingham New Street, with the 10.25 for Paddington, as No 86.248 (later *Sir Clwyd-County of Clwyd*) leaves with the 09.48 for Euston, on 14 May 1975.
Philip D. Hawkins

Above: No 1036 *Western Emperor* skirts the Stratford-upon-Avon Canal at Lapworth with the 14.05 Paddington-Birmingham on 26 February 1975. *Philip D. Hawkins*

Left: No 1056 *Western Sultan* passes Lapworth with the 18.25 Birmingham-Paddington on 12 June 1975.
Philip D. Hawkins

Above right: No 1068 *Western Reliance* passes the Grand Union Canal near Olton with the 06.45 Paddington-Birmingham on the limpid morning of 20 September 1975.
Philip D. Hawkins

Right: No 1023 *Western Fusilier* heads the 'Capitals United Express' Swansea-Paddington railtour through Radley, Oxfordshire, on 5 February 1977.
T. G. Flinders

Left: No 1030 *Western Musketeer* speeds past Bentley Heath crossing, Dorridge, with the 06.45 Paddington-Birmingham on 5 May 1975. *Philip D. Hawkins*

Above: No 1035 *Western Yeoman* viewed from Bentley Heath crossing signalbox as it passes with the 10.25 Birmingham-Paddington on 2 March 1974. *Philip D. Hawkins*

Right: In misty morning sunlight, No 1072 *Western Glory* accelerates away from the Solihull stop with the 06.45 Paddington-Birmingham on 9 October 1975. *Philip D. Hawkins*

Left: An impression of the sheer bulk of a 'Western', as No 1053 *Western Patriarch* climbs up the Bordesley Junction curve, on the approaches to Birmingham New Street, with the 06.45 from Paddington on 4 April 1975. In the background, 47.407 waits at the signal with a freight. *Philip D. Hawkins*

Below: No 1037 *Western Empress* sweeps through Tyseley with the 06.45 Paddington-Birmingham on the misty morning of 19 February 1976. *Philip D. Hawkins*

Right: Maintenance workers are busy repairing vandal-damage at the trackside on 9 April 1975, as No 1030 *Western Musketeer* climbs the Bordesley Junction curve with the 06.45 Paddington-Birmingham. *Philip D. Hawkins*

Below right: No 1051 *Western Ambassador* descends the Bordesley Junction curve to join the main line for Paddington with the 12.25 from Birmingham on 3 May 1975. *Geoff Dowling*

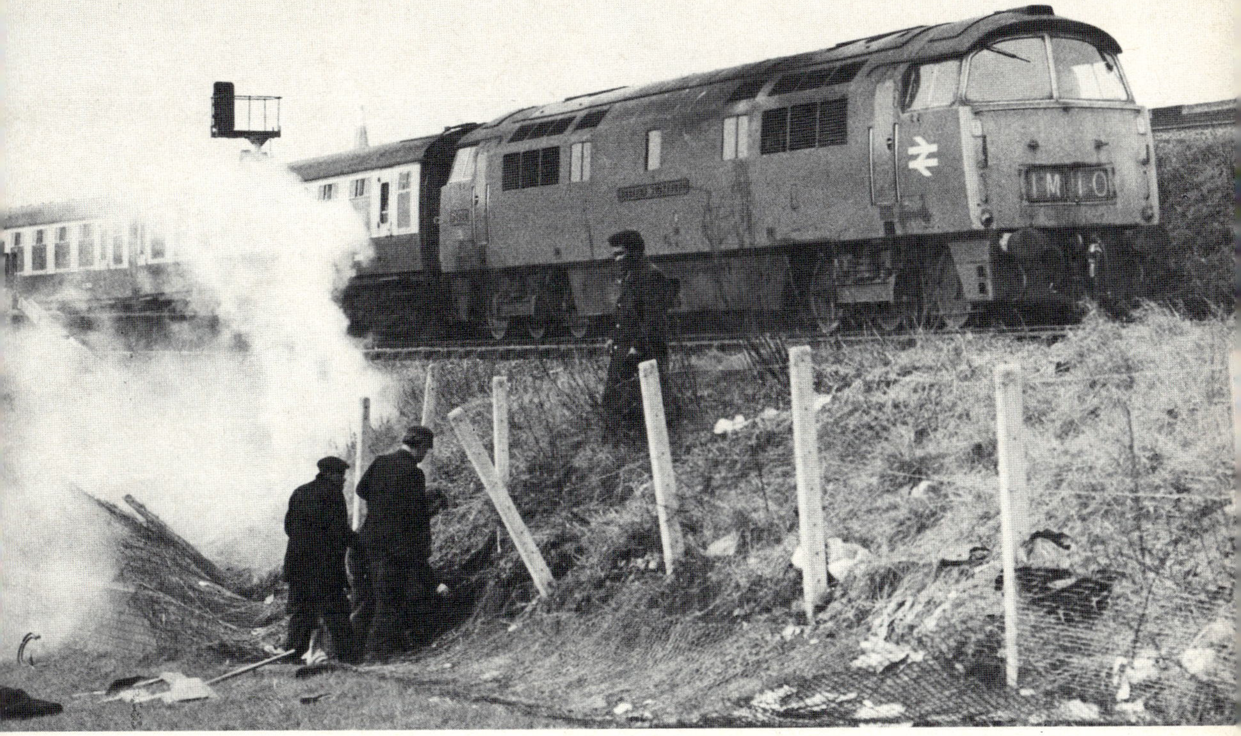
1M10

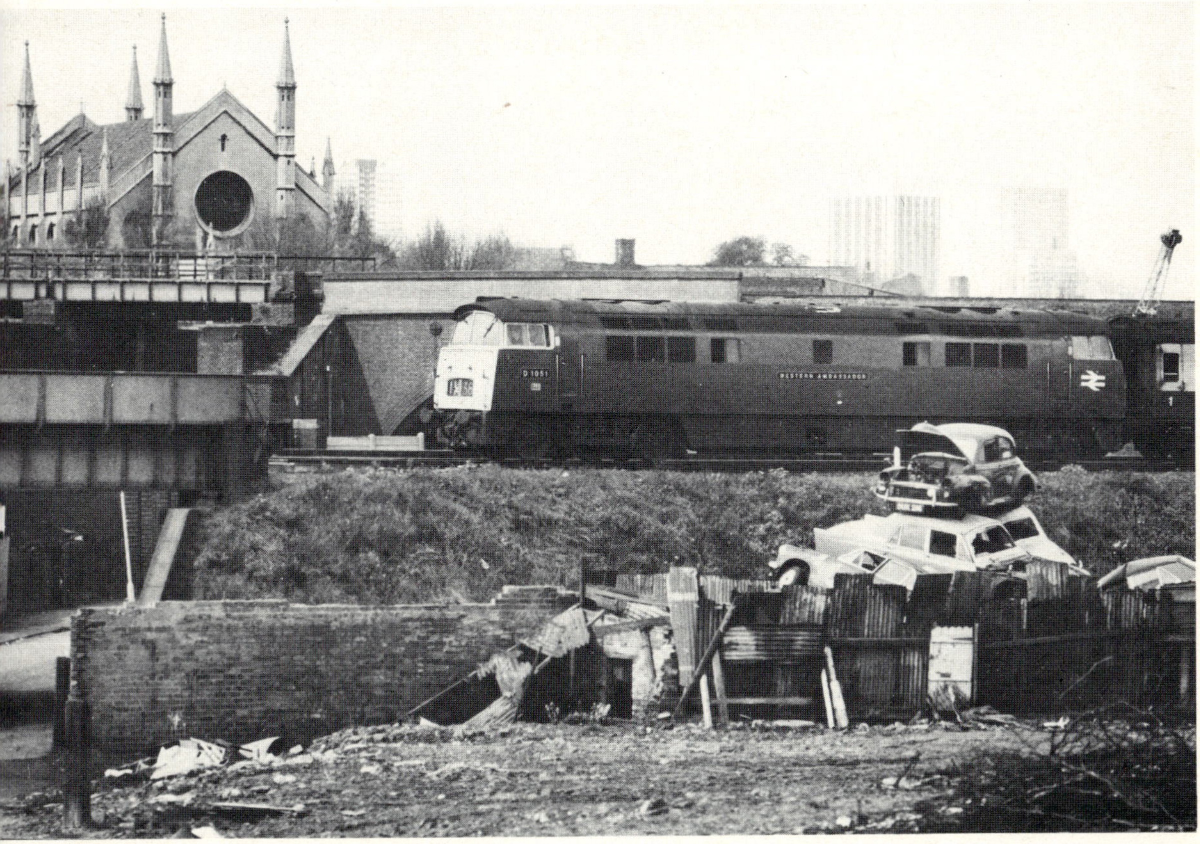
D1051
WESTERN AMBASSADOR

Left: No 1010 *Western Campaigner* skirts the Birmingham-Worcester Canal near Birmingham University with a northbound railtour on 27 November 1976.
Geoff Dowling

Right: An enthusiast moves in for a close-up of No 1013 *Western Ranger* during a photo-stop at Tenby, on the 'Pembroke Coast Express' railtour of 25 September 1975.
A. O. Wynn

Below: On one of the last of the 'farewell' railtours, the 'Southern Belle' of 19 February 1977, No 1013 *Western Ranger* passes Westminster on its departure from Waterloo down the SR main line. *Peter Walton*

Right: Enthusiasts are clustered at the platform-end at Paddington as No 1023 *Western Fusilier* arrives to take out the 'Capitals United Express' railtour on 5 February 1977. *J. A. W. Sykes*

Below: Photographers form a wide arc round No 1023 *Western Fusilier* during a photo-stop at Moreton-in-Marsh on the 'Capitals United Express' railtour of 5 February 1977. *G. Scott-Lowe*

Left: No 1023 *Western Fusilier* pauses for a photo-stop at Swindon, as part of the 'Western Memorial' railtour of 29 January 1977. *J. A. W. Sykes*

Below: No 1013 *Western Ranger* breasts the summit of the Lickey Incline at Blackwell with the northbound 'Merchant Venturer' railtour of 22 May 1976. *John Whitehouse*

Left: On the final day of service of the 'Western' class, 26 February 1977, No 1010 *Western Campaigner* and No 1048 *Western Lady* are acting as standby locomotives for the 'Western Tribute' railtour, at Bristol Bath Road depot. *J. A. W. Sykes*

Below: No 1052 *Western Viceroy*, and No 47.089 *Amazon*, at Old Oak Common locomotive depot on 17 August 1975. *G. Scott-Lowe*

Right: No 1009 *Western Invader* on the wheel-lathe at Cardiff Canton depot on 23 February 1975. *G. Scott-Lowe*

Below right: No 1021 *Western Cavalier* at rest in the running-shed at Laira locomotive depot, Plymouth, on 17 July 1976. *Philip D. Hawkins*

Above: Cabs from No 1001 *Western Pathfinder* and No 1065 *Western Consort* in Swindon Works scrapyard on 23 October 1977. *G. Scott-Lowe*

Below: The hulks of a Swindon cross-country dmu and several withdrawn 'Westerns', No 1003 *Western Pioneer* the most prominent, in Swindon Works scrapyard on 1 May 1976. *R. C. Swift*

Left: Withdrawn 'Westerns' in Swindon Works scrapyard, in appropriately grey conditions in December 1976. *Peter Walton*

Below: The hulks of withdrawn 'Westerns' Nos 1006 *Western Stalwart*, 1035 *Western Yeoman*, and 1003 *Western Pioneer*, in Swindon Works scrapyard on 10 June 1976. *Philip D. Hawkins*

Left: Detail of withdrawn 'Western' No 1031 *Western Rifleman* in Swindon Works scrapyard on 1 May 1976. *Geoff Dowling*

Right: The cab of withdrawn 'Western' No 1031 *Western Rifleman*, viewed from a redundant GWR 'Toad' brakevan in Swindon Works scrapyard on 1 May 1976. *Geoff Dowling*

Below: The hulk of withdrawn 'Western' No 1059 *Western Empire*, with one of its traction bogies in the foreground, and withdrawn Class 24 No 24.075, in Swindon Works scrapyard on 10 June 1976. *Philip D. Hawkins*

Left: Survivors (1): repainted in its original BR maroon, preserved 'Western' No D1062 *Western Courier* is seen at Bridgnorth on a Severn Valley Railway 'Western Day' in 1980. *Bob Morriss*

Below left: Survivors (2): during the Torbay Steam Railway's second 'Western Day', 29 April 1978, No D1062 *Western Courier* eases a Kingswear-bound train over Broadsands viaduct. *Geoff Dowling*

This page: Enthusiasts investigate the remains of No 1028 *Western Hussar* in Swindon Works scrapyard on 28 March 1979. *Kevin Lane*

1028

Survivors (3): for a short period during 1980, preserved 'Western' No D1013 *Western Ranger* ran in a 'desert sand' livery similar to that carried by the very first 'Western', outshopped in 1961. D1013 is seen here at Highley with an afternoon Bridgnorth-Bewdley train on 30 March. *John Whitehouse*